John Wesley

Exemplar of the Catholic Spirit

H. McG.

Herbert Boyd McGonigle

MA, BD, DD, PHD

Former Lecturer at Nazarene Theological College, Dene Road, Didsbury, Manchester, in the classes in Church History, Theology and Wesley Studies, Former Principal of Nazarene Theological College and now Principal Emeritus

© Copyright 2014 Herbert Boyd McGonigle

British Library Cataloguing in Publication Data.
A catalogue record for this book is available from the British Library

ISBN 978 0 86071 683 9

A Commissioned Publication of

MOORLEYS
Print & Publishing
tel: 0115 932 0643 web: www.moorleys.co.uk

FOREWORD

I am delighted that The Revd Colin H Wood ThB MA LTCL, has readily agreed to write this Foreword. A Church of the Nazarene minister and a District Superintendent of the Scotland, Northern Ireland and the North of England until recently, he has shown in the letters he wrote that he had a personal rapport with all his pastors and their people. Colin read my Paper and he agreed that it should be published. He draws attention to what is stated on page 12 that we should pay attention to all that is happening and we should learn from it. I am grateful for Colin's advice and I pray that the Lord's people will mind that too.

"Make every effort to live in peace with all men..." (Heb 12:14). This scriptural exhortation, and others like it – to maintain the unity of the Spirit, to love one another, and even to love our enemies – should characterise the Christian Church is every century. However, Church History often tells a very different story; one of controversy, schism, bitterness, and at times loss of life.

In this little book Dr Herbert McGonigle rediscovers the Catholic Spirit of John Wesley and traces the attempts Wesley made to forge links of fellowship with those who held different views to his own. Surely common courtesy, respect, and fellowship should be possible even if doctrinal positions differ. After all, it was the furtherance of the Gospel and the extension of the Kingdom that was at stake.

The paradox between Wesley's own strongly held views (and his very trenchant statements opposing those who taught differently) on the one hand, and his attempts to find fellowship and common ground with his 'doctrinal opponents' on the other, does sometimes sit a little uneasily. However, the book clearly reveals to us the depth of Wesley's concern and the genuineness of his attempts to seek a unity of spirit and fellowship that would further and not harm the spread of the Gospel.

It is always a happy combination when well researched historical theology is linked to relevant spiritual challenge, and, as in all his writings, Dr McGonigle brings the two together in this publication. As a former pastor, church leader, college principal, church historian and Wesley scholar, Dr McGonigle is well able to bring both the history to our attention and to press home the challenge which results from it. Stories of broken relationships, individually and corporately, among the people of God continue to be heard. Indeed, "All of us who truly long for open, heart-felt and Spirit-inspired fellowship and co-operation among evangelicals in the twenty-first century, must learn from what happened in the eighteenth century." (page 12).

We are grateful for all that has come from the pen of Dr McGonigle over the years and glad that he has been abe to prepare this paper for publication. I warmly commend this book; let us 'read, mark, learn, and inwardly digest' every page. And I trust that the example of this "Exemplar of the Catholic Spirit" of a former century, will cause us, in our day, to search our hearts and be challenged to follow the example of Mr Wesley, for One greater than he taught, "Blessed are the peacemakers" (Matt. 5:9) and prayed, "...that they may be one..." (John 17:11).

Colin H. Wood
Glasgow, Scotland
February 2014

John Wesley

Exemplar of the Catholic Spirit

When John Wesley published this sermon, 'Catholic Spirit,' in 1755, it was much more than merely an addition to his sermon corpus. In content and intention, it expressed Wesley's understanding of what the essentials of Christian experience are and his resolve to work with all those who honoured Christ and promoted his kingdom, even if he differed from them in some doctrinal matters. Earlier he had published another sermon along similar lines, 'A Caution Against Bigotry.' In both sermons Wesley spelt out his warning against the sectarian spirit that divides the people of God and prevents Christians from understanding that God is present and working in fellowships and parties and denominations other than their own. John Wesley has something to say to all of us in the twenty-first century. This contribution will look at what Wesley meant by the catholic spirit and how he practised that spirit in half a century of preaching, writing and setting up the Methodist Societies.[1]

The sermon on bigotry is based on Mark 9. 38, 39, where Jesus cautioned his disciples not to exclude the man casting out demons just because he did not belong to the circle of Jesus' disciples. Wesley defined bigotry as 'too strong an attachment to, or fondness for, our own party, opinion,

---

[1] John and Charles Wesley were responsible for writing and transcribing more that 400 books. John was an omniscient reader and he read all his life up to the end.

1

Church, and religion.'[2] The reference to casting out demons is taken to mean the proclamation of the gospel in the widest sense. The devil has set up his throne in every human heart and it is only the power of Christ, mediated in the gospel, which can evict him. Wesley here assumes a very orthodox understanding of original sin and the deep conviction that the gospel is God's power for our salvation. So the man casting out demons represents all those who fully and faithfully proclaim Christ's gospel. But how, Wesley asks, will we recognise such a man? The test is really quite simple. Have we sufficient proof of a particular man or woman, now unquestionably a Christian, and who was previously a 'gross, open sinner'? If there is also plain proof that this transformation of life came about by hearing a particular preacher, than that preacher unquestionably casts out demons. The point that Wesley wants to make is clear enough – such a preacher is exercising a gospel ministry and we should not hinder him. Having detailed the various ways in which Christians hinder one another because of bigotry, Wesley goes much further. It is not enough merely to tolerate the other preacher and refrain from attaching his methods and party and his particular theological stance; we must positively pray for him and speak well of his ministry. The sermon closes with a very moving appeal:

> Examine yourself.... Do not I hinder sinners from hearing his word?... Search me, O Lord, and prove me. Try out my reins and my heart.... 'Tis well to go this far, but do not stop here. If you will avoid all bigotry, go on. In every instance, whatever the instrument be, acknowledge the finger of God. And not only acknowledge but rejoice in his work, and praise his name

---

[2] *The Bicententennial Edition of the Works of John Wesley* (ed. Frank Baker; 15 vols. Oxford: Clarendon Press/Nashville, Tn: Abingdon Press, 1975-95), II, p. 76. Hereafter cited as Wesley, *Works [BE]*.

2

with thanksgiving. Encourage whomsoever God is pleased to employ, to give himself wholly up thereto. Speak well of him wheresoever you are: defend his character and his mission. Enlarge as far as you can his sphere of action. Show him all kindnesses in word and deed. And cease not to cry to God in his behalf, that he may save both himself and them that hear him.[3]

Most of us will probably have to conclude, to our shame, that there have been too many occasions in the work of God when we have not treated colleagues and our brethren in the way Wesley recommends. Too often we have shown party spirit and an unwillingness to show him or her the true state of our hearts. We have kept quiet and to that extent we have not shown the grace and love that is in our hearts.

A few years later John Wesley published his sermon, 'Catholic Spirit.' He based it on Jehu's question to Jehonadab: 'Is thine heart right, as my heart is with thy heart?' And Jehonadab answered: 'It is. If it be, give me thine hand.'[4] While acknowledging that Jehu was not exactly a model saint, yet Wesley urges that his example here is one that every Christian should imitate. Jehu's question is not about Jehonadab's opinions but about his spirit, his attitude and his affections. How does he regard his neighbour? In a word, is there love in his heart? And then Wesley writes a glorious sentence, pleading that even allowing our differences of opinion, we must not let this stand in the way of brotherly affection: 'Though we can't think alike, may we not love alike?'[5] John Wesley wrote

---

[3] Wesley, *Works [BE]*, II, p. 77.
[4] 2 Kings 10:15.
[5] Wesley, *Works [BE]*, II, p. 82.

much in defence of that understanding of Christian sanctification that he understood as love perfected, and this sentence is as good a practical summary of it as anything he argued elsewhere.

Wesley's sermon goes on to explain that while Christians have different modes of public worship, different ideas about church government and differing practices about the subjects and manner of baptism, yet far more important than any of these is the question: do you love God and all mankind? If you do, then, says Wesley, give me your hand, and I will seek, by God's grace, to love you in His name. This 'catholic spirit' is more important than denominational zeal, or distinctives or any of the outward characteristics of the various 'parties' that make up Christ's church. Where it is found, Christians go forward in God's work hand in hand, and the One great Head of the church is glorified in his people.

Like the sermon against bigotry, this sermon is a call to Christians to put away the party spirit, the unkind criticism, the harsh judgements and the censorious back-biting that Wesley knew only too well to be prevalent in his own day. The first decade of the eighteenth-century revival had witnessed not only strong opposition from many of the clergy of the established church, but bitter controversy inside 'Methodism' itself. Hardly had Wesley's 'field-preaching' begun in Bristol in 1739 when the 'Societies' of the converts were sharply divided over the doctrines of election and predestination. The long-standing friendship begun at Oxford between John and Charles and George Whitefield was strained to breaking point. There were rival claims about who really 'owned' the revival work in Bristol and allegations that John Wesley had usurped Whitefield's rightful leadership. Back in London the Moravians and the 'Methodists' were going separate ways, and the split among the members of the Fetter Lane Society epitomised the growing divide among these former good friends.[6] All these sad divisions, with the accompanying rancour and mutual suspicion, must have been in Wesley's mind when he published this sermon. If only Christians would love one another as their Lord had directed them! There was a great need to call fellow-believers back to the catholic spirit and that was the sermon's intention.

John Wesley knew that however well-intentioned this sermon was, its plea to 'think and let think'[7] could easily be misunderstood for theological and doctrinal indifference. The sermon concluded with a rejection of what Wesley called 'speculative latitudarianism.' This meant uncertainty and indifference about the doctrines of the historic Christian faith. Wesley protested that a man of true catholic spirit is as 'fixed as the sun in his judgment concerning the main branches of Christian doctrine.' Among those who subscribed to the creeds of the church there has always been differences of opinion about ecclesiastical practices and those doctrines that did not affect our salvation. With many of high-Calvinist persuasion, Wesley did not share their opinions about absolute predestination, limited atonement and irresistible grace. Against Roman Catholic's theologians

---

[6] The origins and characteristics of the Fetter Lane Society are very fully discussed in C. Podmore, *The Moravian Church in England, 1728-1760* (Oxford Clarendon Press, 1998), pp. 29-71.

[7] In his 1742 apologetic, *The Character of a Methodist*, Wesley wrote: 'As to all opinions which do not strike at the root of Christianity, we "think and let think."' Wesley, *Works, [BE]*, IX, p. 34.

John Wesley had no place for their teaching on papal infallibility, a propitiatory mass, the adoration of Mary, purgatory and other Roman doctrines. But with protagonists of both Calvinistic and Catholic Christianity, Wesley, while rejecting what he saw as their peripheral teaching, was at one in confessing with them such foundation doctrines as the holy Trinity, the deity of Christ, original sin, justification by faith, holy living and final destiny. But this catholic spirit, which strongly identified with all who asserted the historic doctrines of the faith, was not at all complacent about dangerous diversions.

This was well illustrated in Wesley's response to what he saw as the reductionist Christology of John Taylor of Norwich. A popular Socinian preacher and writer, Taylor published his book *The Scriptural Doctrine of Original Sin, Proposed to Free and Candid Examination*. Written in a lively and very readable style and showing mastery of the biblical languages, it was the eighteenth century's most trenchant attack on the orthodox doctrine of original sin. As a corollary, it undermined the evangelical teaching on justification by faith and, as a pronounced Socinian, Taylor saw Christ as the world's greatest teacher and exemplar of God's grace, but not as God incarnate. As John Wesley itinerated across the four kingdoms of Great Britain, he lamented that Taylor's teaching was producing disciples who ridiculed evangelical Christianity.[8] He waited for some

---

[8]   In his *Journal* for Sunday 28 August 1748, Wesley records his visit to Shackerley in Lancashire: 'Abundance of people were gathered before six, many of whom were disciples of Dr. Taylor, laughing at Original Sin, and, consequently, at the whole frame of scriptural Christianity.' Wesley, *Works [BE]*, XX, pp. 245-246.

orthodox theologian to reply to Taylor, and when none appeared, Wesley took up the cudgels. Retiring for some ten weeks to a friend's house in London late in 1756, he wrote *The Scriptural Doctrine of Original Sin according to Scripture, Reason and Experience* (1757). Running to some 522 pages, it was the single longest treatise that Wesley published.

It was followed two years later by a summary in his sermon 'Original Sin' and there were letters to friends about this controversy, including a letter to Taylor himself. In all these publications Wesley did not attack Taylor in person; indeed he acknowledged that he esteemed his opponent a man of 'uncommon sense and knowledge.' But Wesley had no time for Taylor's Enlightenment optimism about fallen mankind. No writer since Mahomet had given such a wound to Christianity.[9] Wesley unsheathed his controversial sword and threw away the scabbard. What was at stake was nothing less than our 'eternal peace.' The issue between himself and Taylor was, quite simply, 'Christianity or heathenism.' Either he had mistaken the whole of Christianity from beginning to end – or Taylor had. Wesley's scheme – or Taylor's – was as 'contrary to the scriptural as the Koran is.' If the scriptural doctrines of redemption, justification and the new birth are removed, or, alternatively, explained as Taylor explains them, then Christianity is no better than heathenism. If the doctrine of original sin means no more than John Taylor asserts, then Christianity is merely a system of good

---

[9]   *The Letters of the Rev. John Wesley* (ed. J. Telford; 8 vols; London, 1931), IV, p. 48. Hereafter cited as Wesley, *Letters*.

advice and the religion of St Paul has no pre-eminence over the teaching of Socrates or Epictetus.[10]

Having looked at John Wesley's plea for the catholic spirit to prevail among Christians, and noting that it did not mean indifference to plausible heresies, it is time to turn and see how far Wesley exemplified this spirit in his own life and ministry. An appropriate starting point is the year 1739 when Wesley first organised his followers into 'Societies.' Most of these men and women had been awakened by the Methodist preachers and they requested Wesley to help them in discipleship. In this way the Societies were begun and the conditions of membership were simple: 'a desire to flee from the wrath to come, to be saved from their sins.'[11] The rules of these Societies forbade, among other things, swearing, Sabbath-breaking, drunkenness and quarrelling. There were also positive injunctions about doing good, attending the means of grace, studying scripture and family and private prayers. But John Wesley imposed no doctrinal or theological test on those joining the Societies. They might be Calvinists or Catholics, Presbyterians or Moravians, Quakers or Dissenters of any colour - all this made no difference.[12] If their intention was to seek the salvation of their souls, then they were welcome in Wesley's Societies.

Whatever opinions they held about other doctrines, provided these were not the occasion of conflict and controversy, Wesley made them welcome. With the help of his preachers and assistants and class-leaders, he watched over their souls,

---

[10] Wesley, *Letters*, IV, p. 67.
[11] Wesley, *Letters [BE]*, IX, p. 70.
[12] Wesley, *Letters*, IV, p. 297.

preached, taught and explained repentance and faith and then instructed the regenerate to grow in the love of God and man. In a famous passage he said of himself that in life he wanted to know one thing - 'the way to heaven.'[13] Having found it, he spent the rest of his life helping others to find it. Salvation was not in creeds, or dogmas, or styles of worship, or denominational labels, but through faith in the Son of God. Taking the world as his parish,[14] he laboured to help men and women on the way to heaven, for the catholic spirit permitted no barriers among those who practised the love of God and man.

John Wesley's 'United Societies,' as they were called, had been preceded by the Religious Societies. They had come into existence in the late seventeenth century, mostly as the work of Dr Antony Horneck.[15] They, too, catered for those who wanted gatherings where prayer, fellowship and devotional reading were encouraged. But they catered mostly for a religious elite and offered little attraction to those who were not regular worshippers or acquainted with religious matters. In contrast, Wesley's Societies were open and democratic, and their pattern ensured that they were geared to help those who were mostly strangers to religious practices, forms and terminology. Indeed many of these early 'Methodists' were illiterate and the Societies

---

[13] Wesley, *Works [BE]*, I, p. 105.
[14] Wesley, *Works [BE]*, XXV, p. 616.
[15] Antony Horneck (1641-97), came to England from Bacharach in Germany in 1661. In about 1678 he began to organise meetings for young men in and around London in order that they 'might apply themselves to good discourse and to things wherein they might edify one another.' See J. S. Simon, *John Wesley and the Religious Societies* (London, Epworth Press, 1921), p. 10.

introduced them not only to the essentials of Christian doctrine but also spurred them to learn to read and write.

In the late 1730s and early 1740s, the Methodists were divided by wrangles over election and predestination. An anonymous letter circulated among the converts in Bristol warning them not to listen to John Wesley because he preached against predestination. Although the accusation was false, the rumours spread and finally Wesley preached and then published his sermon, 'Free Grace.' It was a strong attack on absolute predestination but no names were mentioned. George Whitefield replied with his *A Letter to the Rev. Mr John Wesley* (1740), censuring him for publishing a provocative sermon, and then attacked Wesley's theology. The outcome of this doctrinal quarrel among former friends was that the revival split into two groups; those who followed the Wesley brothers were designed Wesleyan Methodists and those who sided with Whitefield and his supporters became known as Calvinistic Methodists. This 'parting of the ways' among old friends hurt both parties and it bred mistrust and suspicion of fellow believers on both sides.

The record of this early, and lasting, breach in the work of the eighteenth century revival constitutes a sad and depressing chapter. While this historic divide, usually but inaccurately, labelled the Calvinistic/Arminian dispute, had been part of Evangelicalism since the seventeenth century, its resurrection among the eighteenth century Methodists can never be an occasion of rejoicing for the evangelical historian or theologian. Former friends went their separate ways, fellowships were broken off, misunderstanding and half-truths proliferated and the work of God and evangelism suffered. If only John Wesley and George Whitefield had come together and, even if complete doctrinal were not possible, surely there could have been a brotherly rapport that eclipsed discord and allowed the glorious work of soul-saving to prosper. Looking at both camps, with Whitefield, John Cennick and their supporters on one side, and the Wesley brothers and their preachers on the other, what potential there was to advance the work of God. What might have been achieved if these good and godly people had been catholic enough in spirit to agree to disagree on some theological interpretations in order to support each other in evangelising the land.

Writing to Whitefield in the midst of the warfare, John Wesley acknowledged that it was bigotry that divided the evangelicals.

> The case is quite plain. There are bigots both for Predestination and against. God is sending a message to those on either side. But neither will receive it, unless from one of his own opinion. Therefore for a time you are suffered to be of one opinion and I of another. But when His time is come God will do what man cannot – namely, make us both of one mind.[16]

Over the next few years this dispute rumbled on and there was also a gap opening up between John Wesley and the Moravians. Ever since he had first met the Moravians on a voyage to America in 1738, John Wesley had been profoundly influenced by their teaching and example of holy living. His ties with them in Georgia were very strong, and

---

[16] Wesley, *Letters*, I, p. 351.

when he returned in 1738, he and Charles formed a close friendship with the Moravian Peter Bohler. The progress of the Wesleys' spiritual pilgrimages between February and May 1738 was directed by the counsel and teaching of Bohler and it climaxed at Pentecost that year. Charles Wesley found the assurance of sins forgiven on Pentecost Sunday while staying in a Moravian home in London. Three days later a similar experience of 'heart-warming' came to John while attending a Moravian gathering. His record of what happened that Wednesday evening in Aldersgate Street was couched in Moravian language: 'I felt my heart strangely warmed. I felt I did trust in Christ, Christ alone for salvation, and an assurance was given me ...'[17]

The Wesley brothers and the Moravians worked together very closely in London and later in 1738 John Wesley visited the Moravian headquarters in Herrnhut in Germany and met the founder, Count Zinzendorf and other leaders. When his itinerant preaching ministry began in Bristol in April 1739, he had the full support of the Moravian brethren and his many letters to James Hutton, a leading English Moravian, shows how close this friendship was. Differences began to emerge when a German Moravian, Philip Molther, introduced 'Stillness' practices into the Fetter Lane Society. This teaching advocated that seekers after God should refrain from all the means of grace, including scripture reading, prayer and hearing sermons, and wait for the Spirit to bring to them the gift of faith. The Wesleys opposed this emphasis, convinced that through these means of grace God mediated his Spirit to bring people to repentance and faith.

---

[17] Wesley, *Works [BE]*, XVIII, p. 250.

There was a split in the Fetter Lane Society and a large number followed the Wesleys out of that Society and joined with them in a new fellowship, the first of the many Wesleyan Societies that would be organised in the years ahead.[18]

Although the Wesleys and the Moravians still shared some love-feasts together, there was disagreement among them on the question of the believer's sanctification. With their strong Lutheran background, the Moravians emphasised the imputation of Christ's righteousness to the Christian. Increasingly the Wesleys, while advocating imputation, were also stressing the transforming work of the Spirit in the Christian's life and spoke of imparted or inherent righteousness as well. The Christian is not only accounted righteous but he is being made righteous. This emphasis convinced John Wesley that the Moravian teaching, unless it was expressed very carefully, opened the door to antinomianism. This dispute with old friends who esteemed each other highly might well have been amicably resolved but for the intervention of Count Zinzendorf. On a visit to London in 1741 he met with John Wesley and was totally unsympathetic to any notion of imparted holiness. James Hutton's biographer later recorded that Zinzendorf openly disparaged what he called the Wesleys' 'self-made holiness.' In his capacity as 'bishop and guardian of the Church of the Brethren,' he publicly branded John and Charles Wesley as

---

[18] The Wesley brothers and their followers began to meet at the Foundery, a building which they purchased in the Moorfields district of London. The Foundery became the headquarters for the Wesleys' work for almost forty years. See *The Journal of the Rev. John Wesley* (ed. N. Curnock; 8 vols. London: Epworth Press, 1938), II, pp. 316-319. Hereafter cited as Wesley, *Journal*.

'false teachers and deceivers of souls' and declared that fellowship between the Moravians could only be restored if the Wesleys dropped their delusions about 'Christian perfection.'[19]

It was John Wesley's growing unhappiness about these divisions between the three groupings of the revival movement that led him to propose a conference of all the parties in an attempt to heal the breaches. He took the initiative to call leaders together in London in August 1743. George Whitefield responded positively and Howell Harris likewise. Harris, a recognised leader of the revival work in Wales, was a close friend of both Whitefield and the Wesleys and a man of a truly catholic spirit. Although his theological persuasions put him closer to Whitefield than to the Wesleys, both parties regarded him with warm affection.[20] Charles Wesley recorded that he was itinerating in Cornwall when John asked him to attend the conference. Whitefield, Harris and the Wesley brothers convened but the Moravians were not represented. John Wesley invited one of their leading preachers, August Spangenberg, an old friend of his from their days together in Georgia, but just before the conference was due to start, Spangenberg left England for America. This was a blow to John Wesley's high hopes that the gathering would resolve differences among brethren and bring about a closer co-operation in the work of evangelism and building up the work of God. The reason for the Moravians' refusal to take part was their condition that the

---

[19] D. Benham, *Memories of James Hutton* (London, 1856), p. 112.

[20] Arnold Dallimore suggests that a very friendly letter from Harris to John Wesley in May 1743 may well have prompted Wesley's decision to call a conference. A. Dallimore, *George Whitefield* (2 vols; Edinburgh: Banner of Truth, 1979-1980), II, p. 145.

Archbishop of Canterbury should be informed of the proposed meeting and that an Anglican bishop should be invited. Charles Wesley wrote of his disappointment when he arrived in London and heard that the meeting had been cancelled.

There is clear evidence that John Wesley was deeply disappointed that the divisions among the Methodists and between the Moravians and Methodists had not been resolved. Out of a 'strong desire to unite with Mr Whitefield as far as possible' and to 'cut off endless dispute,'[21] he had proposed some modifications in his own doctrinal emphases. He reasoned that the two sides were divided over three main points; unconditional election, irresistible grace and final perseverance. He would accept a doctrine of unconditional election for some, provided it did not entail the necessary damnation of all the rest. Nor would he object to an interpretation of irresistible grace, unless it implied that those on whom it worked without apparently producing any response were therefore irrevocably damned. As to final perseverance, Wesley went even further in trying to effect a harmonious unity among leaders of the revival. He confessed that he believed there was a state of grace from which the Christian could not fall away.

On any scale of measurement Wesley's olive branch was a remarkable gesture. In the history of theological disputes among Christian theologians, there are few examples of those who have been willing to moderate previously-held views for the sake of co-operation and brotherly affection.

---

[21] Wesley, *Works [BE]*, XIX, p. 332.

Far more often these disputes have led to protagonists hardening their attitudes, and, it is to be feared, also their hearts. John Wesley knew that many would interpret his proposals as a 'climb down' on his part, but there is no doubt that he genuinely wanted to be reconciled with Whitefield. He published this remarkable theological *eirenicon* in his *Journal* for all to see. Given the time of its composition, it looks as if John Wesley had prepared these propositions for the hoped-for conference in London. Sadly, nothing came from these proposals. John Wesley had taken considerable steps to bring old friends together and even though they failed, they were welcome examples of the catholic spirit.

Five years later there were still some lingering hopes that even now Whitefield and Wesley might yet establish some kind of union in the work of the revival. Whitefield had been to America for four years and on his return wrote to both the Wesleys, expressing the hope that they would meet him in London. John Wesley was preaching in the north of England and Charles was in Ireland. Whitefield wrote another letter to John Wesley, expressing disappointment that they had not been able to meet in London and then asked Wesley if he had any further thoughts about union. Whitefield confessed that he felt he and Wesley were on 'two different plans.'[22] His own 'attachment' to America did not allow him to stay long in England and he expressed fears that even if he formed societies here he had no 'proper assistants' to take care of them. He hoped that he and Wesley would meet soon and in the meantime he asked for his prayers, assuring John that he esteemed him 'most affectionately.'

---

[22] Wesley, *Works [BE]*, XXVI, p. 327.

While Whitefield's letter seemed to discourage any move towards a union of his people and Wesley's, yet the tone was warm and friendly and it breathed good will. In the hope of yet establishing a closer relationship with Whitefield, John Wesley proposed a meeting in Bristol. It was another olive branch in another attempt to settle differences and bring the leaders of the revival closer together. On Wednesday 2 August 1749, John and Charles met with George Whitefield and Howell Harris in the Wesleyan 'New Room' in Bristol. The first day was spent in discussing how they might establish 'a closer union in affection.' They agreed not to believe rumours about each other, to defend the other's reputation and not to speak about difference of opinion in a way that caused friction. Agreement was reached after 'some mild and friendly debate' on an understanding of justification. The next day predestination and perfection were on the agenda. Again there was a general spirit of agreement, particularly mentioning that both sides agreed, on the predestination question, not to use 'such terms as naturally tend to revive the controversy.' There was further harmony in agreeing that terms like 'sinless' and the 'inbeing of sin' should be dropped and all Christians should be exhorted to 'press on to perfection in the holy love of God.'[23]

While this meeting of the four Methodist leaders seemed very promising in the agreements reached, it is difficult to gauge what good came from it. John Wesley made no record of it in his *Journal* and this might be the best indicator that

---

[23] 'An Early Methodist Eirenicon,' *Proceedings of the Wesley Historical Society 5* (1905), pp. 108-10.

the outcome was disappointing. Charles Wesley made a brief mention of the gathering in his *Journal*, saying that it 'came to nought, I think through their flying off.'[24] If this is an accurate observation on the conference, then certainly Charles Wesley felt that if Whitefield and Harris had been willing to stay longer in discussion, much more might have been achieved. Having convened the 1743 gathering in London and this meeting in Bristol six years later, John Wesley might well have felt he had done his utmost to bring about reconciliation. While the Bristol gathering seems to have concluded in good will and with mutual affection, it did not bring the parties together in doctrinal harmony over the disputed matters of predestination and Christian perfection.

The history of Methodism shows only too clearly that the theological divisions continued to be subjects of polemics for the decades to come. John Wesley had certainly displayed a truly catholic spirit and both Whitefield and Harris seem to have responded in kind. But it must be said that so much more could (and should) have come from those gatherings of the evangelic leaders. Perhaps what was needed was an acknowledgement by Wesley and Whitefield that their published wrangling ten years earlier had had melancholy consequences. If both leaders had acted with less haste in vindicating their own positions, later hostilities might have been avoided. If only John Wesley had not gone to the printers with his trenchant sermon, *Free Grace*! And if George Whitefield had directed his *Letter* to Wesley in private, rather than publishing it! All of us who truly long for open, heart-felt and Spirit-inspired fellowship and co-

---

[24] *The Journal of the Rev Charles Wesley* (2 vols; London, 1849), II, p. 63.

operation among evangelicals in the twenty-first century, must learn from what happened in the eighteenth century. The catholic spirit certainly means that we will not attack and criticise one another openly, nor will we have any part in allowing unfounded rumours to make us suspicious of one another. But the catholic spirit also means that whatever convictions we hold personally on the questions of predestination, perfection theories, gifts of the Spirit, women in ministry, and such like, we will pray for, support and work with all those who believe and proclaim the great doctrines of historic orthodox Christianity.

By the late 1740s, John Wesley found himself taking care of a rapidly-growing number of people who had joined his Societies in their search for salvation. To help them in that quest and confirm those already in the way of salvation, Wesley instituted class meetings, band meetings, love-feasts, quarterly meetings and other such means of grace. Full-time preachers were recruited, assistants and local leaders were appointed and a circuit system was set up. John Wesley also began to compose, extract from other works, edit and publish many writings for the instruction of his preachers and the edification of his people. These publications ranged from popular evangelistic tracts like, *A Word to a Swearer*, *A Word to a Drunkard, A Word to a Sabbath-Breaker* and *A Word to a Smuggler,* to reasoned apologetics like, *An Appeal to Men of Reason and Religion* (1743), *A Further Appeal to Men of Reason and Religion* (1745), and *A Plain Account of Christian Perfection.* In 1749 he began a very ambitious publishing project. This was his *Christian Library*, fifty duodecimo volumes, subtitled, *Extracts from and Abridgements of the Choicest Pieces of Practical Divinity which have been Published in the English Tongue.* Believing that 'reading Christians will be knowing Christians,'[25] he edited extracts that began in the first century with Clement of Rome and extended to works written in the eighteenth century.

Wesley concentrated on what he called 'practical divinity;' those writings that were meant to confirm the Christian faith and build up believers in holy living. In his own words, this *Christian Library* would constitute 'Christianity reduced to practice.'[26]

> I have endeavoured to extract such a collection of English Divinity, as (I believe) is all true, all agreeable to the oracles of God: as is all practice, unmixed with controversy of any kind; and all intelligible to plain men: such as is not superficial, but going to the depth, and describing the height of Christianity. And yet not mystical, nor obscure to any of those who are experienced in the ways of God.... I take no author for better, for worse; (as indeed I dare not call any man Rabbi) but endeavour to follow each so far as he follows Christ.[27]

This *Christian Library*, a huge literary undertaking for a busy, travelling preacher, is a good guide to John Wesley's understanding of both Christian truth and Christian practice. The *Christian Library* demonstrates how Wesley's hermeneutic, in a typical Anglican way, was constituted by scripture, tradition and reason. But there was a fourth dimension to this approach to Christian theology and practice – and that was experience. Wesley was sure that the

---

[25] Wesley, *Letters*, VI, p. 201.
[26] Wesley, *Christian Library* (50 vols;1749-55), II, p. 3.
[27] Wesley, *Christian Library*, I, p. ix.

'experience' of sins forgiven and the indwelling Christ were privileges granted to Christians in every age. The *Christian Library* was intended not only as an instructor in Christian truth but also a means of confirming Christian practice and encouraging what Wesley often summarised as true Christian experience – the 'faith that works by love' (Gal. 5.6). John Wesley's *Christian Library* was yet another illustration of his deep commitment to the catholic spirit. When the contents of the *Christian Library* are examined carefully, it gives a remarkable insight into the scope and depth of Wesley's Christian sympathies. The extracts represent the Apostolic Fathers, continental authors, Anglican and Puritan writers and some anonymous devotional writing. The Fathers are represented by Clement of Rome, Polycarp, Ignatius and Macarius. Wesley's appreciation of the fourth century Macarius is typical of his penchant for practical Christian instruction.

> Whatever he insists upon is essential, is durable, is necessary. What he continually labours to cultivate in himself and others is, the real life of God in the heart and soul, that kingdom of God, which consists in righteousness, and peace, and joy in the Holy Ghost. He is ever quickening and stirring up in his audience, endeavouring to kindle in them a steady zeal, an earnest desire, an inflamed ambition, to recover that Divine image we were made in; to be made more conformable to Christ our Head; to be daily sensible more and more ...[of] such a victorious faith as overcomes the world, and working by love, is ever fulfilling the whole law of God.[28]

If Wesley's inclusion of the writings of Macarius in his *Christian Library* does not provoke much surprise, it is

---

[28] Wesley, *Christian Library*, I, p. 71.

different with the writings of two medieval Roman Catholic writers. They were Antoinette Bourignon (1616-80), a Spanish Quietist, and Miguel de Molinos (1640-97), also a Spanish Quietist. While John Wesley took a vigorous stand against Roman Catholic doctrines, such as transubstantiation, purgatory, indulgences, papal infallibility and all forms of martyrology, yet he was willing to recognise that some Catholic writers were helpful in promoting practical Christianity. Although he was later castigated by Richard Hill and Augustus Toplady for promoting popery, Wesley defended his use of these writers. Whatever the deficiencies in their understanding of some Christian doctrines, they had deep, personal acquaintance with Christ through his Spirit. Both were exponents of a kind of meditative spirituality that placed great emphasis on waiting on God, and little of what could be described as distinctive Roman dogma was found in their pages. Wesley also made it plain that when he selected an extract from any particular book, it did not mean that he agreed with everything else in that volume, much less what that author might have written elsewhere. In compiling the *Christian Library*, Wesley made it plain that he was an editor, not the author. Wesley's attitude to these Catholic mystics is well summarised in the preface he wrote in his extensively-edited *Life* of Madam Guyon. She was a French Catholic mystic and a self-confessed disciple of the writings of Molinos.

> The following contains all that is scriptural and rational; all that tends to be genuine love to God and our neighbour. In the mean time, most of what I judge to be contrary to Scripture and reason is omitted ....The grand source of all her mistakes was this; the not being guided by the written word. She did not take the Scriptures for the rule of her actions; at most it was but the secondary rule. Inward

impressions, which she called inspirations, were her primary rule. The written word was not a lantern to her feet, a light in all her paths....Yet with all this dross, how much pure gold is mixed! So God did wink at involuntary ignorance...[29]

Given John Wesley's well-known predilection for Anglican authors, especially those of the Restoration period, 1660-1700, the inclusion of extracts from their writings would be expected in his *Christian Library*. And they are there, including Thomas Ken, Jeremy Taylor, Simon Patrick, William Cave, John Tillotson, William Beveridge and many more. But there are just as many Puritan authors represented in his *Christian Library*. And the list of names is impressive, including Richard Sibbes, Thomas Goodwin, Richard Alleine, Richard Baxter, Edmund Calamy, John Flavel, John Howe and others. Indications of the high esteem in which John Wesley held these and other Puritan writers can be found scattered throughout all his publications, and in the *Christian Library* he gave specific reasons for including them. He was not blind to what he believed to be both their literary and theological imperfections, but their practical value more than compensated for these weaknesses.

> They are exceeding verbose, and full of circumlocutions and repetitions. But I persuade myself, most of these defects are removed in the following sheets ...But it should not be concealed, there are other blemishes in the greater part of the Puritan writers. They drag in controversy on every occasion, nay, without any occasion or pretence at all. Another is, that they generally give a low and imperfect view of sanctification or holiness.... But abundant recompence is made for all their blemishes, by the excellence which may be observed in them....Their

---

[29] Wesley, *Works*, XIV, pp. 276-77.

judgement is generally deep and strong, their sentiments just and clear, and their tracts on every head full and comprehensive…. More particularly they do exalt Christ. They set him forth in all his offices…. And next to God himself, they honour his Word. They are men mighty in the Scriptures, equal to any of those who went before them, and far superior to most that have followed them…. They are continually tearing up the very roots of Antinomianism…. But the peculiar excellency of these writers seems to be, the building us up in our most holy faith.[30]

Among the Puritan writers from whom Wesley extracted material for his *Christian Library* were some whose high Calvinism he had little sympathy with. But here he followed the same principle as when he made extracts from medieval Catholic writers; an extract did not necessarily mean Wesley's agreement with other parts of the writing. In both these examples, Wesley was putting the catholic spirit into practice. If the writer exalted Christ and, in particular, promoted practical holiness, then his or her attachment to doctrines not acceptable to Wesley was no bar to his using the 'good grain.' With references to the English Puritans, Wesley's use of the writings of John Owen demonstrates that for him the catholic spirit took precedence over personal opinions. Owen was unquestionably the most dogmatic Calvinist of the English Puritans and his book, *The Death of Christ,* was the most extensively-argued presentation of his doctrine of limited atonement that could be found. He was, not unnaturally, a vigorous exponent of the doctrine of absolute predestination and did not shy away from the doctrine that consequently flows from it – reprobation. To

---

[30] Wesley, *Christian Library*, IV, pp. 106-107.

John Wesley, any concept of the doctrine of reprobation was utterly irreconcilable with his understanding of the love of God. He vehemently rejected the doctrine of unconditional election because 'it necessarily implies unconditional reprobation. Find out any election which does not imply reprobation, and I will gladly agree to it.'[31]

Although Owen was the acknowledged defender of high Calvinist doctrines, yet Wesley included extracts from Owen's writings in his *Christian Library*. When he used the Catholic mystics, he carefully avoided any extracts that promoted Catholic doctrine or mysticism. Likewise with his use of Owen. From the many volumes of Puritan works, Wesley avoided all controversial matter, and selected what was calculated to glorify Christ and incite the Christian to holy living. He made use of four of Owen's publications. They were his *Mortification of Sin in Believers*, *Of Temptation, the Nature and Power of it*, *A Declaration of the Glorious Mystery of the Person of Christ, God and Man*, and *Of Communion with God the Father, Son and Holy Spirit*. In these writings the Christian met with 'practical divinity.' Wesley could recommend these works to every Christian seeking instruction in scriptural truth and guidance on the holy life. Wesley's catholic spirit prompted him to include extracts from the writings of this magisterial Calvinist theologian, but extracts that carefully avoided what Wesley considered to be unhelpful, and often confusing, theological speculation.

Two more examples of John Wesley's catholic spirit are worth noting. In 1749 he published *A Letter to a Roman*

---

[31] Wesley, *Works*, X, p. 211.

Catholic. It acknowledged that Protestants and Roman Catholics held many prejudices about each other but it was not opinions on either side, or a particular mode of worship, that made a man a true Christian. All those who call themselves Protestants but in practice are 'common swearers, drunkards, whoremongers, liars ....in a word, all who live in open sin,' are really heathens. The true Protestant worships God in spirit and truth, loves God and his neighbour and walks in holiness. Wesley then challenges his Roman Catholic reader. Can he find fault with this description of a Christian? Is he following Christ in like manner? Is his whole life a sacrifice to God and is he delivered from both outward and inner sin? 'This, and this alone is the old religion. This is true, primitive Christianity. O when shall it spread over all the earth! When shall it be found both in us and you? Without waiting for others, let each of us, by the grace of God, amend one.'[32] Wesley then proceeded to offer a remarkable *eirenicon* of Christian good will to Roman Catholics.

> Are we not thus far agreed? Let us thank God for this, and receive it as a fresh token of his love. But if God still loveth us, we ought also to love one another.... I hope to see you in heaven. And if I practice the religion above described, you dare not say I shall go to hell. You cannot think so....Your own conscience tells you the contrary...Then if we cannot as yet think alike in all things, at least we may love alike.... Let us resolve to harbour no unkind thought, no unfriendly temper, towards each other. Let us lay the axe to the roots of the tree; let us examine all that rises in our heart, and suffer no disposition there which is contrary to tender affection...O let you and I press on to the prize of our high calling, that being justified by faith, we may have peace with God

---

[32] Wesley, *Works*, X, p. 85.

through our Lord Jesus Christ; that we may rejoice with in God through Jesus Christ, by whom we have received the atonement; that the love of God may be shed abroad in our hearts by the Holy Ghost which is given unto us.[33]

John Wesley was seeking what common ground he could find between Roman Catholics and himself. He was making a very important distinction between Roman Catholic dogma, which he repudiated, and Roman Catholic people whom he loved for Christ's sake. Their dogmas were 'a heap of erroneous opinions delivered by tradition from their fathers.'[34] The true gospel of salvation by faith had effectively driven popery out of England and that gospel alone could keep it out.[35] Wesley openly declared that he 'detested and abhorred the fundamental doctrines of the Church of Rome,'[36] but his attitude to Roman Catholic people was one of good will, concern for their bodies and souls, and a ready acknowledgement that in character and conduct many of them gave indisputable evidence of being true Christians.[37] Here again there is testimony of how John Wesley endeavoured to distinguish between opinions and true faith. He was as forthright as any eighteenth century English Protestant in exposing what he believed to be the numerous and dangerous errors of Roman Catholicism but his love for his neighbour warmly and genuinely embraced Roman Catholicism. Throughout his ministry he strongly maintained that there is a very important distinction between essential Christian doctrine and personal opinions. There can

---

[33] Wesley, *Works,* X, pp. 85, 86.
[34] Wesley, *Works*, VI, p. 199.
[35] Wesley, *Works [BE]*, I, p. 129.
[36] Wesley, *Works*, I, p. 456.
[37] Wesley, *Works*, III, p. 312.

be no compromise on vital doctrines but opinions are another matter. He spelt it out in a letter to John Newton in 1765. 'You are admirably well expressed what I mean by an opinion contradistinguished from an essential doctrine. Whatever is "compatible with a love for Christ and a work of grace" I term an opinion.'[38]

Our final look at how John Wesley demonstrated the true catholic spirit is concerned with his hopes for a practical working unity among England's evangelical clergy. Following a friendly meeting in March 1761 with Henry Venn, vicar of Huddersfield, Wesley took positive steps towards bringing about a fraternal union among evangelical ministers. Writing to George Downing, an Essex rector, he spoke about how he had laboured for many years 'to unite, not scatter, the messenger of God.' Now he voiced the hope that all those who embraced essential Christian doctrines might come together in a kind of harmonious unity that would greatly enhance the work of God.

> I think it great pity that the clergymen in England who preach the three grand scriptural doctrines- Original Sin, Justification by Faith, and Holiness consequent thereon – should have any jealousies or misunderstanding between them. What advantage must this give to the common enemy! What a hindrance is it to the great work wherein they are all engaged! How desirable is it that there should be the most open, avowed intercourse between them! But surely, if they are ashamed to own one another in the faces of all mankind, they are ashamed of Christ, they are ashamed of Him that sends if they dare not avow whom He has sent…. For many years I have been labouring after this – labouring to unite, not scatter, the messengers of God…. As God has enabled

---

[38] Wesley, *Letters*, IV, p. 297.

me to stand almost alone for these twenty years, I doubt not but He will enable me stand either with them or without them.[39]

Three years later John Wesley took this plan for unity among the evangelical clergy a step further. He wrote a letter to almost fifty of the leading evangelical clergy in the Church of England, including George Whitefield, William Romaine, John Newton, Walter Shirley, Henry Venn and John Berridge. The plea was for a coming together of all those who were 'fellow labourers in his gospel.' Wesley reasoned: 'Ought not those who are united to one common Head, and employed by Him in one common work, be united to each other?' After naming those he wished to unite, Wesley added that this proposal included any other clergy who agreed on the doctrines of original sin, justification by faith and holiness of heart and life.[40]

Wesley then set out the kind of union he had in mind. It was not a unity of opinions, or expressions or outward order; rather a unity of good will and mutual support. Hindrances would be removed when ministers did not judge or envy each other, were not displeased with others who had greater success than they had, and did not gossip about the faults, mistakes and infirmities of their brethren. But Wesley was concerned that this evangelical fraternity would be marked, not only by its avoidance of critical and judgmental attitudes, but positively by the way it manifested the fruits of the Spirit. These brethren would love, think well of and honour each other. They would speak respectfully of one another,

---

Wesley, *Letters*, IV, p. 146.
[40] Wesley, *Works [BE]*, XXI, p. 456.

defend each other's characters and help one another in every possible way. It would require an earnest effort on the part of all concerned to desire this unity, and it would require the grace and power of God working through them to accomplish it.

> All nature is against it, every infirmity, every wrong temper and fashion; love of honour and praise, of power, of pre-eminence; anger, resentment, pride, long-contracted habit, and prejudice lurking in ten thousand forms. The devil and all his angels are against it. For if this takes place, how shall his kingdom stand? All the world, all that know not God, are against it, though they may seem to favour it for a season. …. But surely 'with God all things are possible.' Therefore 'all things are possible to him that believeth.' And this union is proposed only to them that believe, that show *their* faith by *their* works.[41]

John Wesley was deeply disappointed that most of the clergy to whom he wrote did not even bother to reply to him. Just as he had done in early years in trying to bring the Methodist and Moravian preachers together, now he was attempting to unite the evangelical clergy in the Church of England. He longed for a unity of purpose and vision among his brethren that would strengthen their united efforts in evangelism and in building up the work of God. His vision and hope and prayer was that the catholic spirit might characterise all those who truly loved God and their neighbour. As he repeatedly said: 'If we cannot think alike, then at least let us love alike.' If that catholic spirit was needed among the people of God in Britain in the eighteenth century, it is needed no less in this twenty-first century. And it is fitting that this attempt to demonstrate what John Wesley meant by the catholic spirit

---

41 J. Wesley, *Works [BE]*, XXI, pp. 457, 458.

should conclude with words by his brother Charles, words expressing that what unites us in Christ is far more important than our denominational labels or our theological slogans.

Sweetly now we all agree
Touched with softest sympathy
Kindly for each other care
Every member feels its share.

Love, like death, hath all destroyed
Rendered all distinctions void
Names, and sects, and parties fall
Thou, O Christ, are all in all.[42]

---

[42]   G. Osborn (ed.), *The Poetical Works of John and Charles Wesley* (13 vols; London, 1868-72), I, p. 362.

Books by Revd Dr Herbert Boyd McGonigle

William Cooke on Entire Sanctification, Beacon Hill Press, Kansas City, Missouri, 1978.

The Arminianism of John Wesley, Moorleys Print & Publishing, Ilkeston, Derbyshire, 1988.

John Wesley and the Moravians, Moorleys Print & Publishing, Ilkeston, Derbyshire, 1995.

John Wesley's Doctrine of Prevenient Grace, Moorleys Print & Publishing, Ilkeston, Derbyshire, 1995.

Scriptural Holiness: The Wesleyan Distinctive, Moorleys Print & Publishing, Ilkeston, Derbyshire, 1995.

Sufficient Saving Grace: John Wesley's Evangelical Arminianism. 350 pages, Paternoster Publishing, Carlisle, Cumbria, 2001.

To God Be The Glory: The Killadeas Convention 1952-2002, Moorleys Print & Publishing, Ilkeston, Derbyshire, 2002.

John Wesley's Arminian Theology: An Introduction. Moorleys Print & Publishing, Ilkeston, Derbyshire, 2005.

A Burning and a Shining Light: The Life and Ministry of William Bramwell. Moorleys Print & Publishing, Ilkeston, Derbyshire, 2009.

Christianity or Deism? John Wesley's Response to John Taylor's Denial of the Doctrine of Original Sin. Moorleys Print & Publishing, Ilkeston, Derbyshire, 2012.